INCREDIBLE OCEAN!

Eye-opening Photos of

Life Underwater

playBac
PUBLISHING
More.Brain.Power

Oceans are incredible! They are home to an amazing variety of plants, animals, and habitats.

In the following pages, you will find leaping whales, heaping turtles, sneaky eels, and learn fascinating facts about starfish, jellyfish, flatfish, viperfish, and many aspects of ocean life that are not fish at all!

These photos have been selected for their energy, emotion, and fun. They are an invitation to a fabulous voyage deep under the sea, and to amazing discoveries— each more surprising than the last.

Turn the page to begin your trip around the world, and to learn about ocean life from a whole new perspective.

Fakarava is an island within the Tuamotu Archipelago, French Polynesia, in the Pacific Ocean—the largest chain of atolls in the world. (Atolls are high sandbars built upon coral reefs.) The beautiful and species-rich reefs make these islands some of the most scenic underwater destinations on the planet. Visitors can see many species such as the kingfisher, mantis shrimp, barracuda, and tiger shark. Fakarava is part of a UNESCO classified biosphere, reserved to maintain this fragile ecosystem and to promote a balanced relationship between humans and the world around them.

Teamwork!

Bottle-nosed dolphins often work as a team to hunt for schools of fish. Each dolphin has a signature whistle, or squeak, that is unique among the group and helps them communicate with each other. They are known for their friendly character and curiosity toward humans. Sometimes they cooperate with local fisherman by driving fish toward their nets, and eating any leftovers that don't get caught. Now that's teamwork!

An icy treat for a Sea Star.

This sea star (also known as a starfish) is devouring an ice-covered bush sponge in Antarctica. There are over 2,000 species of sea star living all over the world— from tropical habitats to the coldest regions. Most have the remarkable ability to consume prey outside their bodies! Their stomachs emerge from their mouths, envelope the meal, and withdraw back inside the sea star's body. A very tricky way to get a snack!

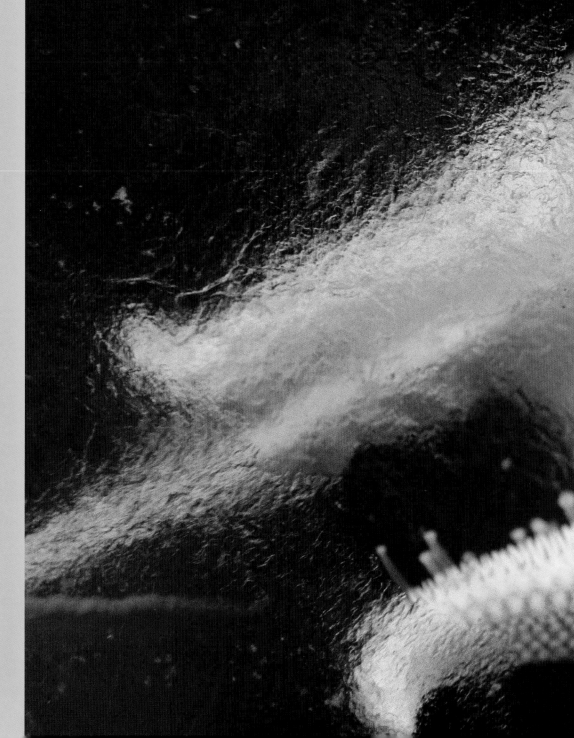

Sea dragon or Seaweed?

Sea dragons can be found in seaweed beds, sea grass meadows, and kelp gardens. Can you guess why? They have the perfect camouflage, of course! Their bodies are surrounded by protective plates that closely resemble their habitats, and long, tubular snouts give them the appearance of tiny dragons. Although they do not have teeth and are not very good swimmers, they are not easy to catch because they can be so difficult to see!

A very mellow shark.

This epaulette shark seems content to relax on the ocean floor. That's because this species of shark is a "bottom-feeder," and that's where his food is! He sometimes uses his fins to "walk" on the floor of a tide pool in search of prey. Relatively small—only 15 to 25 inches in length—epaulette sharks are very sluggish and quite harmless.

A different kind of comet!

Starfish (also called sea stars) have amazing powers of regeneration. Some starfish, like the Linckia, can replicate (regrow) themselves from only one arm. When a predator tears off one of its arms, that arm will slowly grow into a completely new starfish. The new star begins life with four tiny arms attached to the old arm, resembling a shooting star.

what's for lunch?

The North Pacific giant octopus can weigh up to 33 pounds, with an arm span of up to 14 feet! It is a very intelligent animal, capable of unscrewing jar lids in order to get at food. But when it comes to eating, this octopus doesn't worry about containers! It eats shrimp, clams, crabs, scallops, abalones, fish—such as this spiny dogfish—and even other octopuses!

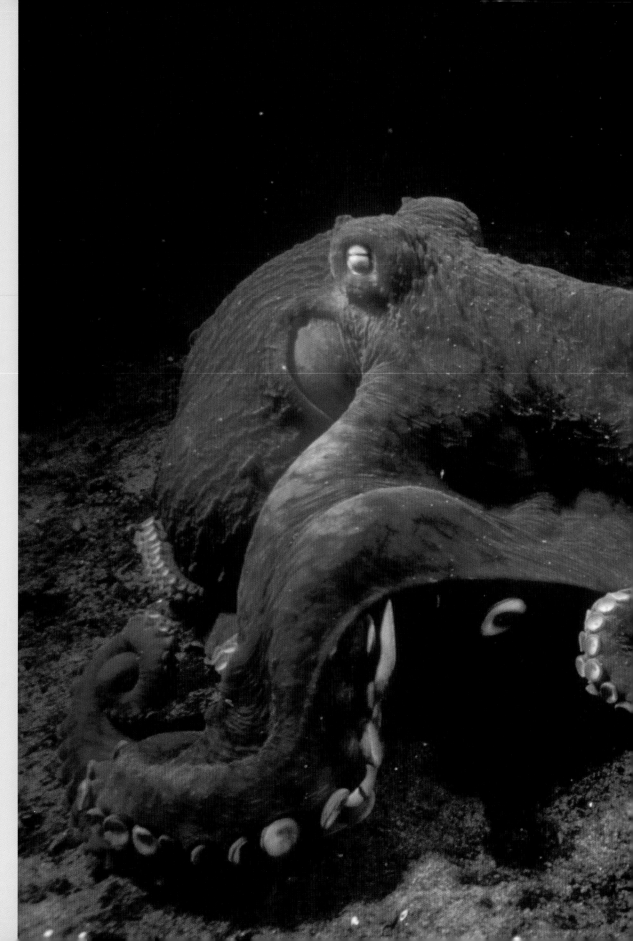

Gotcha!

The oceanic whitetip shark is not a fast swimmer, but it is capable of quick bursts of speed when feeding. They generally prefer deep, open water but occasionally are found close to shore. Reaching lengths from 10 to 13 feet, this aggressive fish has attacked more humans than all other shark species combined! Watch out for the whitetip!

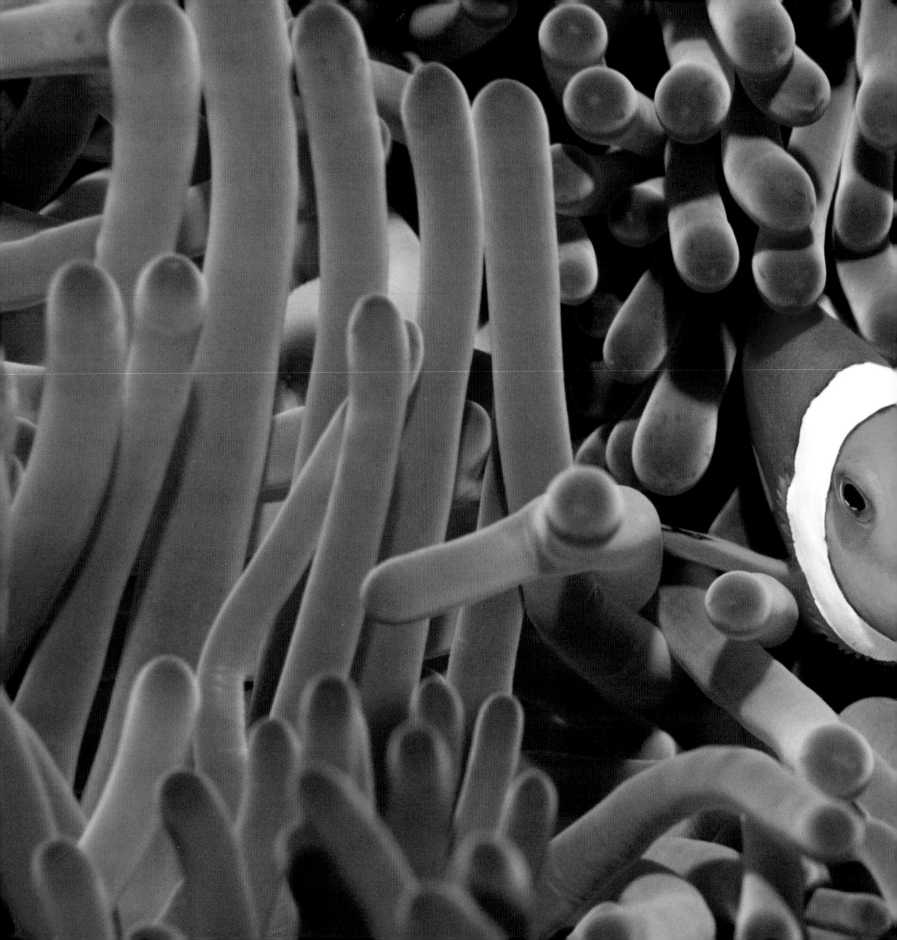

No clowning around!

The clown anemonefish is known by its orange color and three bands of white encircling its body. It has a very close relationship to its home, the anemone. The anemone provides shelter, and the clown anemone fish provides protection against turtle and fish attacks in return. Strangely enough, this fish is usually a very poor swimmer, and the anemone usually stings anything that comes near it. Alone they are not very successful, but together they are quite a team!

who's afraid of the moray eel?

Reaching up to nearly six feet in length, the green moray eel is capable of eating an octopus whole! But bad table manners are the least of its problems. These eels have no scales on their skin, and are covered entirely by slimy, yellow mucus! The mucus, when seen atop their brownish-gray skin, provides the eerie green glow for which they are named. Tricky camouflage or a scary Halloween costume?

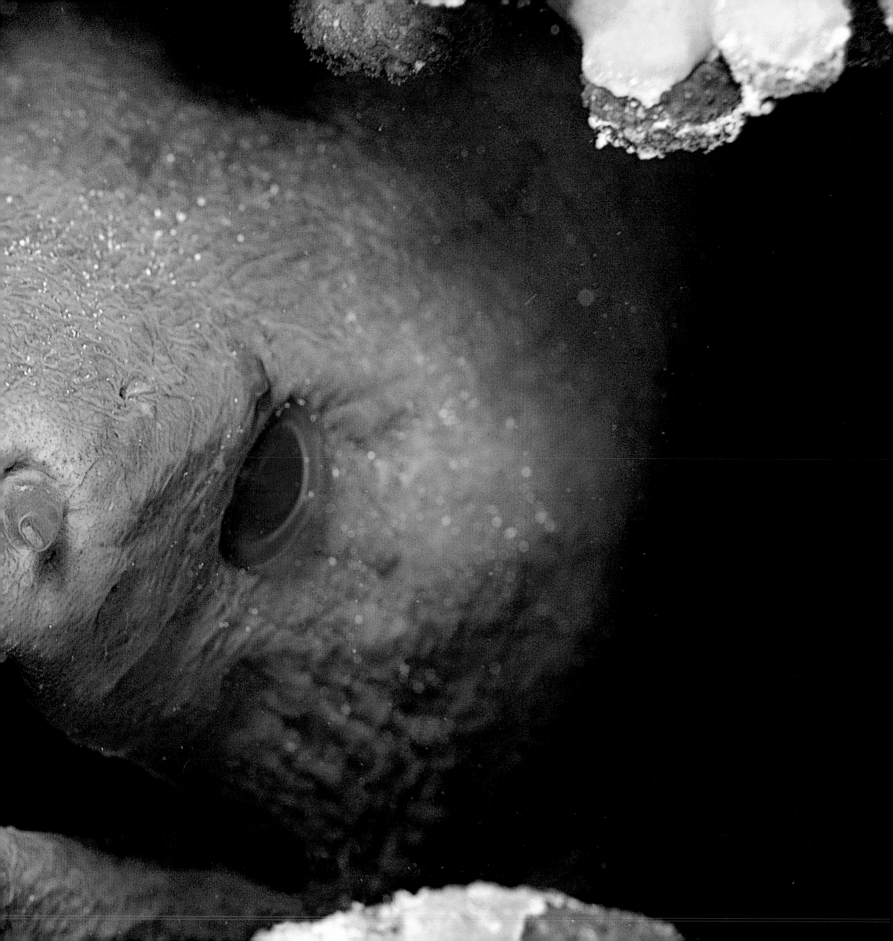

The giant humpback whale is a water taxi for tiny barnacles.

Weighing nearly 40 tons (up to 79,000 pounds!) and reaching lengths of 40 to 50 feet, humpback whales can host a lot of barnacle passengers. These small animals live in very hard shells that become embedded in the skin of the whale. Acorn barnacles, which prefer slow-moving rides to faster ones, such as on dolphins, are the most common species found on humpback whales. One such humpback was found to have over 900 pounds of acorn barnacles attached to it! That's a heavy load!

Hello there!

The most recognizable feature of the bottle-nosed dolphin is his elongated snout (his "bottle nose"). However, this is not a true nose; it is his mouth. The bottle-nosed dolphin actually breathes through a blowhole located on top of his head, and rises to the surface two or three times per minute to do so. Perhaps they should be called "bottle-mouthed dolphins"!

Pretty . . . and pretty dangerous!

The peacock mantis shrimp rarely reaches lengths over six inches, but it can produce forces that are thousands of times its body weight! Primarily green, with orange leopard-like spots, they are attractive enough to earn the name "peacock." But when hunting, they use the heel of their "arm" to smash prey to bits with extraordinary force, striking so quickly that water actually vaporizes in the wake of their movement!

May I have this dance?

Tiger tail seahorses are poor swimmers, but they're great dancers! Although they are technically fish, they do not have scales and they do not swim headfirst, but in an upright position. While courting, they move side by side, hold tails—or grip a strand of sea grass together—and wheel around in what is known as their "predawn dance."

Don't talk with your mouth full!

The yellowstriped cardinalfish is a tiny fish that lives in lagoons and reefs. Only two to three inches long, they live in groups under ledges, in holes, and even among the spines of sea urchins! The protective father cardinalfish holds the eggs safely in his mouth until they are ready to hatch. What a mouthful!

The chambered nautilus is a "living fossil."

The chambered nautilus can withdraw completely into its shell, closing the opening with a flap formed by two folded tentacles. In order to swim, it draws water into and out of its living chamber. This pumping movement allows the nautilus to move up and down. They can live up to 20 years—a very long time for a mollusk!—and have remained relatively unchanged for millions of years.

A midnight snack for soft coral.

Alcyonarian coral is a tree-like colony of soft, translucent animals. Coral reefs are made up of millions of these animals—called "polyps"—that are related to sea anemones and jellyfish. Reefs begin when a polyp attaches itself to a rock on the sea floor and then divides into thousands of clones, creating a colony that acts as one organism. At night, the polyps open to grab nutrients—and sometimes even small fish—for their midnight snack.

A pile up of loggerhead sea turtles!

A loggerhead sea turtle can live up to 50 years, growing to an average length of 36 inches and weighing up to 300 pounds! During the winter months they migrate to tropical waters, where the males wait for the females offshore from nesting beaches. Once hunted for their meat, eggs, and shells, the loggerhead sea turtle is now internationally protected.

What are you looking at?

The shortnose batfish lives on flat sandy bottoms, in sea grass beds, or in mud. Without a doubt, it is one of the strangest-looking fish in the sea. Batfish do not have scales. Instead, they are covered in rough, wart-like bumps. Their front fins are on arm-like stalks that are used to walk along the ocean floor. If approached by a human, the batfish will freeze, stock-still, hoping to go unnoticed.

This parrot can swim!

Parrot fish teeth are arranged along their jawbones to form a hard, beak-like structure. Like the colorful birds they are named for, they use their "beaks" to collect food, which consists of algae and polyps from the coral reefs. To keep from being eaten, the parrot fish secrete a thick mucus to mask their own scent from predators, such as the moray eel.

A male pharoah cuttlefish closely guards his mate.

He may not be able to walk like an Egyptian, but this cuttlefish is capable of swimming by jet propulsion. By drawing water into its body cavity and then quickly expelling it, he can move rapidly through the water. Very aggressive protectors, cuttlefish will block the den of the female until she has laid her eggs, and raise their arms in a defensive position to ward off rivals.

The scalloped hammerhead shark has one great sniffer!

Hammerhead sharks are like giant swimming noses. They move their heads from side to side to "smell" the water as they swim. The strange shape of their heads may actually increase the hammerhead's sight and smell abilities. Because their eyes and nostrils are separated further than any other shark species, they can detect chemicals, the scent of wounded prey, and even weak electrical fields in the water.

A white-spotted rose anemone attacks an egg-yolk jelly!

Anemones, cousin of the jellyfish, remain in one place for their entire lives, stuck to rocks by strong suction cups. They will eat just about any animal that comes close enough to be caught. Averaging two feet in diameter, the translucent jelly is yolk yellow at its center and has dozens of tentacles, some trailing as long as twenty feet. Although it sounds like a messy meeting, this large jellyfish is usually found drifting motionless and is easy prey for the anemone.

At home among the coral.

The Banggai cardinalfish are vigorously territorial and have highly developed homing skills. They quickly retreat to the location of their family or school when threatened by predators, but they may not be quick enough! Prized for fish tanks and home aquariums, they may soon be placed on the endangered species list due to over collection.

Open wide!

The leopard seal is curious, bold, and powerful. Its unusually loose jaw can open more than 160 degrees, allowing it to bite very large prey, including emperor and king penguins. The leopard seal's eyesight and sense of smell are highly developed, making it a formidable predator, and—at close to 1,000 pounds—a heavyweight hunter as well!

"Crunch" goes the sea urchin!

The wolf eel has a large, square head and powerful jaws—both necessary to obtain its favorite foods: sea urchins, clams, and mussels. These eels also have canine teeth, which give them a wolf-like appearance. Although they are pretty fearsome-looking—and can grow up to 80 inches long—wolf eels are not aggressive toward humans.

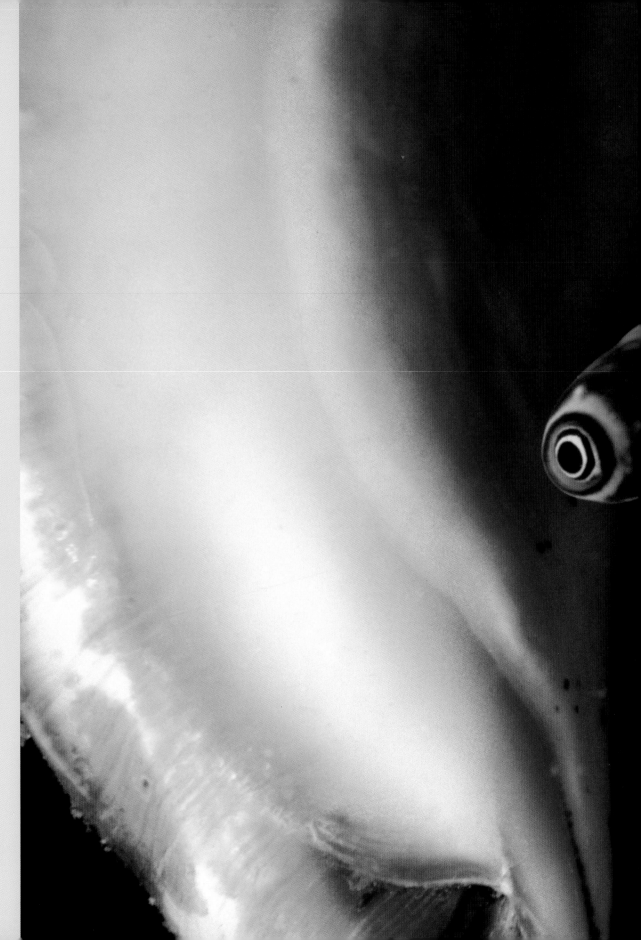

The queen conch peeking out of her shell.

A long-lived species, these conch have an estimated life span of up to 40 years! The adult shell can be up to twelve inches long and weigh as much as five pounds. Prized for its edible meat and beautiful pink-lined shell, the queen conch is a victim of over-fishing, which has become a serious concern.

West Indian manatees—more playful than they look!

Although manatees—or sea cows—can weigh up to 3,000 pounds, they are surprisingly agile in the water, performing somersaults, circular rolls, and occasionally swimming upside down! They are capable of moving freely between freshwater and salty marine habitats, where they consume 5–10 percent of their body weight in food each day! Two hundred-pound lunch, anyone?

It's an anemone ... It's a giant crab ... No, it's the mimic octopus!

Growing up to two feet in length, the mimic octopus can copy the appearance and movements of more than fifteen different species, including stingrays, seashells, lionfish, sea snakes, mantis shrimp, and anemones. The mimic chooses who to impersonate depending on which predators are nearby. It can even imitate large jellyfish by swimming to the surface, spreading its arms, and slowly sinking back to its home on the sandy ocean bottom. Quite a show!

Dinnertime for reef sharks at the surface.

The Caribbean reef shark is one of the largest predators at the top of its food chain. Their sharp senses of smell, hearing, sight, and touch help them hunt large crabs, reef fish, and rays. Prey is snatched quickly at the side of the shark's mouth in a sudden snap of the jaws. No one is going to tell the reef shark not to swallow his dinner whole!

61

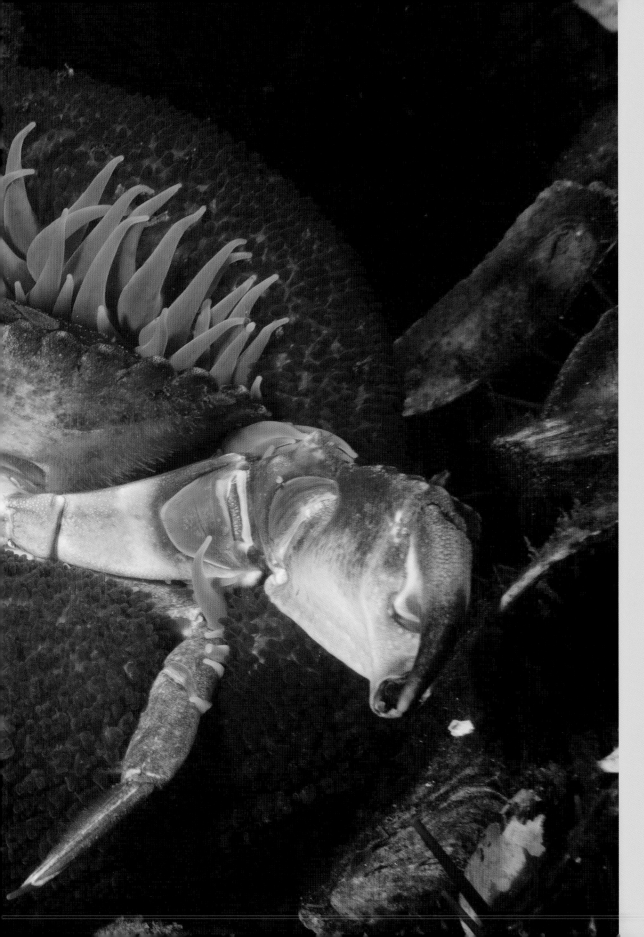

A red cancer crab struggles to survive the grip of a giant green anemone.

Red crabs live on a diet of barnacles, sea cucumbers, and dead fish, but they make a tasty treat for green anemones! The anemone and its tentacles are a deep green color due to the algae that live within it. The algae are protected from other grazers inside their hosts, while the anemone gains extra nutrients from their guests. In these rocky tide pools, it's eat or be eaten!

63

The potato cod is one soggy spud!

The large, dark brown, potato-shaped markings along its body give this cod its peculiar name. Extremely territorial and very aggressive toward intruders, the potato cod can grow up to six feet long! They ambush their prey by hiding behind coral and darting out to quickly grab their meal. The mouth of the potato cod is so big, they eat their prey—even octopus and lobster—in one big gulp!

Pucker up! The mantle of a giant clam.

Once known as a man-eating clam, the giant clam is no longer considered to be particularly dangerous. Although they reach weights of over 400 pounds and lengths as much as 4 feet across, giant clams subsist on plankton and the proteins produced by the billions of algae that live inside them. The multi-colored mantel is the clam's soft shell lining. It is exposed while these gentle giants filter plankton from the surrounding water.

A Halloween mask on the ocean floor.

The whitemargin stargazer is rarely seen. That's because it spends most of its time buried in sand or mud, remaining motionless, and staring directly up—hence the name "stargazer." Despite its pretty name, this fish is venomous and has two poison spines above its front fins. The stargazer's favorite trick is to dangle a lure that resembles a tasty worm—but is actually a fleshy attachment on the bottom of its mouth—to get the attention of smaller fish it is waiting to snap up for dinner.

The flamboyant nudibranch struts his stuff!

Nudibranchs are any marine mollusks that do not have shells or gills. They come in a variety of bright, intense colors that warn predators to stay away. If their showy colors aren't enough to dazzle enemies, nudibranchs can release toxic slime that is sour and repellant to any predator unfortunate enough to take a bite. As you can imagine, not many animals are foolish enough to eat a nudibranch!

Surf's up!

Gentoo penguins stand about 28 inches high and have a relatively long tail, which just might help stabilize their surfing moves. They are superb swimmers and can hold their breath for dives lasting up to seven minutes. But gentoo penguins really set the record when it comes to speed: They are the fastest underwater swimming penguins, reaching speeds of 22 miles per hour!

Ambush in an ice cave!

These red sea stars (or starfish) live in the very cold waters off Antarctica, where they are the most abundant sea star in the region. Although primarily red in color, the red star can actually be pale pink, purple, or orange. They have a strange and varied diet that consists of dead fish, sea sponges, seal poop, and even other sea stars!

This sea walnut can glow in the dark!

Sea walnuts are also known as "warty comb jellies." They are small—only three to five inches long—warty, and have transparent bodies. The "combs" that run along the length of the sea walnut glow blue-green when the animal is disturbed. Although it is related to jellyfish, the walnut does not sting.

One huge belly flop!

Humpback whales live in groups, called pods, and migrate seasonally, from the tropics in winter to northern feeding grounds in summer. Although they can weigh up to nearly 40 tons (79,000 pounds!), humpbacks are agile and acrobatic swimmers, leaping out of the water and slapping back down with a mighty splash. They also breach the water while feeding in a speedy move designed to shovel as many fish as possible into their mouths.

The northern feather duster worm: afraid of the dark?

When the tide goes out, feather duster worms look like clusters of pencils standing at attention. Their feathery red and green plumes open to collect food and oxygen from the water only when they are completely covered by the sea. The tentacles of its plumes are light sensitive and when a shadow falls across the worm, they quickly snap back into the tube!

cowabunga!

Adult male polar bears weigh between 660 and 1,760 pounds, but that doesn't stop them from taking the plunge! In fact, they are excellent swimmers who can travel widely underwater in search of food. Their paws are broad enough to serve as paddles in the water, and they have thick fur that provides insulation and traction for walking on snow and ice. Polar bears are well equipped for life in and near the water.

A harlequin crab, perfectly camouflaged on a sea cucumber.

Harlequin crabs can reverse their spots from brown with white spots to white with brown spots, depending on the sea cucumber they are living on! The crabs have a friendly relationship with the cucumbers (so named for their elongated shape), which allows them to hide from predators and search for food while remaining relatively unnoticed in their near-perfect camouflage.

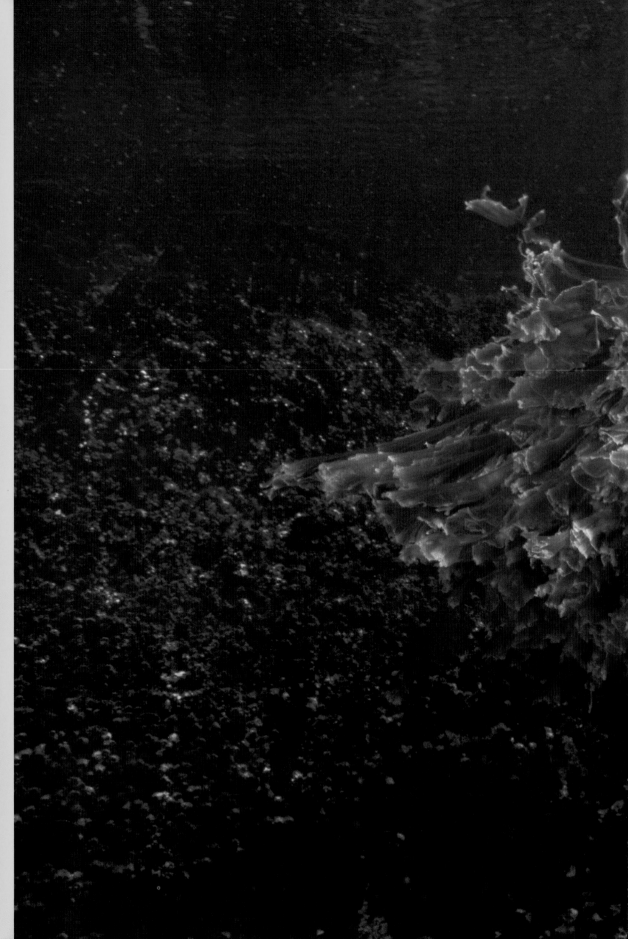

Lion's mane jellyfish: deadly even when dead!

The lion's mane is the largest known species of jellyfish, capable of reaching a diameter of 8 feet, with tentacles trailing as long as 100 feet or more! It catches zooplankton, small fish, or other jellyfish by encircling its prey in very sticky tentacles. Dinner is captured in this net of tentacles and stunned by specialized cells that sting and eventually kill. Watch out! Even a dead lion's mane jellyfish or a detached tentacle is capable of stinging!

Beware the puffer fish!

Puffer fish are found near shore in shallow seas. They have rough skin and are clumsy swimmers. But they are known for their famous defense mechanisms: the ability to ingest huge amounts of water and turn themselves into spiny balls, and a deadly toxin that lives in their internal organs. Although some predators, like tiger sharks, seem unaffected by this poison, humans are not so lucky: There is enough toxin in one puffer fish to kill 30 adult humans!

Viperfish are some of the fiercest predators of the deep!

The sharp, fang-like teeth of the viperfish are too large to fit in its mouth! Instead, they curve backward toward its eyes. The lower jaw is longer than the upper and carries a series of pointed teeth set far apart. It uses these deadly teeth to impale its victims by swimming toward them at high speeds. These shrimp-like mysids don't stand a chance!

Lettuce coral, not fit for salads!

Also known as "bowl coral," "octopus coral," and "pagoda cup coral," lettuce coral has a hard skeleton that is covered with a thin, velvety skin. The base color is usually yellow, or yellowish-green, due to photosynthesis occurring within the algae that lives on the coral. This Turbinaria species of coral is actually carnivorous (a meat eater), feeding on bits of shrimp, mysids, and zooplankton.

Index

All photos © Getty Images.

Special Thanks to:

John Candell, Christopher Hardin, Cheryl Weisman, Jacleen Boland, and Paula Manzanero

on the cover:

The lionfish, also known as the dragon fish, scorpion fish, or turkey fish, is one of the most poisonous fish in the world. Its venomous spines, sharp as needles, are deadly to prey. Although these spectacularly striped spines and fins make the lionfish a truly incredible example of ocean life, they're sending only one message: Beware!

Copyright 2009 by Play Bac Publishing USA, Inc.

ISBN: 978-1-60214-084-4

Play Bac Publishing USA, Inc.
225 Varick Street
New York, NY 10014-4381

infospbusa@playbac.fr
Contact number : +12126147725

Printed in Singapore

Distributed by Black Dog & Leventhal Publishers, Inc.
151 West 19th Street
New York, NY 10011

First Printing 2009

April/2009